One-Minute

BIBLE

DEVOTIONS

Christine A. Dallman

Publications International, Ltd.

Christine Dallman is a freelance writer living in Everett, Washington. Previously she has worked as an editor for Cook Communications and is the coauthor of *How to Let God Help You Through Hard Times* and the author of *Daily Devotions for Seniors*.

Cover Photos: Brand X Pictures; Getty Images

Louis Weber, CEO
Publications International, Ltd.
7373 North Cicero Avenue
Lincolnwood, Illinois 60712

ISBN-13: 978-1-4127-1572-0
ISBN-10: 1-4127-1572-5

Manufactured in U.S.A.

8 7 6 5 4 3 2 1

CONTENTS

IT ONLY TAKES A MINUTE...

Not many of the prayers recorded in the Bible are long and drawn out. Most biblical prayers are petitions that go right to the heart of the matter. Even our Lord's model prayer for his disciples is brief and simple enough for a young child to learn. Jesus, in fact, prefaced that prayer with the following instruction: "When you are praying, do not heap up empty phrases as [some people] do; for they think that they will be heard because of their many words. Do not be like them, for your Father knows what you need before you ask him" (Matthew 6:7–8).

So if the idea of a "mere" one-minute prayer seems somehow inadequate or irreverent, have no fear! Scripture makes it quite clear that it is the quality of our prayers, not the quantity of our words, that matters to our Lord. That is to say, the best prayers come not from an eloquent tongue but from a sincere heart.

One-Minute Bible Devotions is designed to help you explore biblical prayers of psalmists, prophets, kings, apostles, and saints. Each prayer is followed by a brief meditation and a short prayer you can use as your own or as a starting point for your personal prayers. Whether you're sitting down for quiet time or needing a bit of inspiration on the go, this little book will turn your heart toward God in a fresh attitude of prayer.

Do not worry about anything, but in everything by prayer and supplication with thanksgiving let your requests be made known to God. And the peace of God, which surpasses all understanding, will guard your hearts and your minds in Christ Jesus.
Philippians 4:6–7

Help & Deliverance

❧ ❧ ❧

LIGHT IN THE DARKNESS

Indeed, you are my lamp, O Lord, the Lord lightens my darkness. . . . You have given me the shield of your salvation, and your help has made me great. You have made me stride freely, and my feet do not slip.

2 Samuel 22:29, 36–37

Being in darkness can be frightening: not knowing what is around us, where to step, whether there is danger. How much more frightening when we do not have the lamp of God's presence illuminating the darkness of our personal uncertainties! As we walk in faith, however, God himself lights our way, revealing what is unseen, guiding us in the way we should go and keeping us from harm until we are safely home.

Lord, be with me today and always, I pray. I need your presence lighting my way through an often dark world. Thank you for your light; in you there is no darkness.

POWER FOR THE POWERLESS

O Lord, there is no difference for you between helping the mighty and the weak. Help us, O Lord our God, for we rely on you, and in your name we have come against this multitude. O Lord, you are our God; let no mortal prevail against you.

2 Chronicles 14:11

Sometimes the "multitude" we face is a multitude of pain, a multitude of trouble, a multitude of opposition from others, a multitude of sadness, a multitude of ...? When it feels as though there is a multitude of something that is too big for us, threatening to distress us, what can we do? There is only one who is bigger and more powerful than anyone or anything else in life. Let us remember today that our God is for us, and his power is greater than that of any multitude.

My Lord and my God, in you I stand today against the multitude that would seek to discourage my faith. In every circumstance that threatens to overwhelm me, please grant me your peace as you exercise your power to protect me.

Prayer at Sunrise

Lord, in the morning you hear my voice; in the morning I plead my case to you, and watch.

Psalm 5:3

Upon waking, dozens of thoughts clamor to encroach upon our peace of mind: our list of to-dos, an unresolved conflict, the money we need that hasn't arrived yet. All the odds and ends of living come rushing back upon us like little leeches seeking to drain the life out of us. Before our feet even hit the floor, nagging troubles can eclipse the initial joy we felt at seeing sunlight dancing on a wall, hearing a bird chirping outside, or having a purring cat curled at our feet. Turning our thoughts toward heaven each morning, calling on God, and placing our cares in his capable hands are how we can battle back, recover joy, and hit the floor in good spirits because we know God is in control.

Heavenly Father, cause me to turn my thoughts to you each morning before I begin grappling with life's issues on my own. Help me fight for peace and joy by praying for your help and finding strength in you.

CARRIED BY THE SHEPHERD

The Lord is the strength of his people; he is the saving refuge of his anointed. O save your people, and bless your heritage; be their shepherd, and carry them forever.

Psalm 28:8–9

As grown-ups, we're not fond of the idea of "being carried"; it implies a helplessness, a loss of independence, and a feeling of imposition on others. Simply stated, it calls up our greatest fears and ravages our last line of dignity. Children are carried, not adults! But Jesus said that the kingdom of heaven is made up of those who are most like children—of those who will surrender to their need to be carried by God. In his arms, our fear and pride melt away. In his arms, we rest in the true source of strength. In his arms, we find what it means to have childlike faith. In his arms, we are saved.

Great Shepherd, as I surrender to my need for you, let my soul feel your strength lifting and enfolding me. Carry me today and always, I pray.

Saved From Self-Made Messes

Evils have encompassed me without number; my iniquities have overtaken me, until I cannot see; they are more than the hairs of my head, and my heart fails me. Be pleased, O Lord, to deliver me; O Lord, make haste to help me.

Psalm 40:12–13

Oh! It's agonizingly hard to "come clean" when one bad choice has led to another and has snowballed out of control. But we have a merciful God. We have a God who does not chide those who turn to him with a sincere heart of repentance. No matter how far down the road of self-sufficiency we've wandered, he's just behind us, ready to embrace us if we'll just turn around and ask him to lead us back in the right direction.

Merciful Lord, when my self-sufficient ways lead me into trouble, help me turn around to find your mercy.

TROUBLED WORLD, TRUSTING HEART

God is our refuge and strength, a very present help in trouble. Therefore we will not fear, though the earth should change, though the mountains shake in the heart of the sea; though its waters roar and foam, though the mountains tremble with its tumult.

Psalm 46:1–3

Global warming, wars, drugs and crime, families falling to pieces. Whatever we might add or take away from this list, we don't need to look far to see that our world is a tumultuous, trouble-filled place. What should we do if the world itself collapses? The psalmist had an answer, and it did not include fear. Come what may, God is our protection, our provision, our "very present help in trouble."

Lord, this world is full of trouble, but you have told us not to be afraid. Help me act in faith without fear. "I believe; help my unbelief" (Mark 9:24)!

SAFE UNDER HIS WINGS

O God, you are my God, I seek you .... For you have been my help, and in the shadow of your wings I sing for joy. My soul clings to you; your right hand upholds me.

Psalm 63:1, 7–8

It is said that in a grass fire, a prairie chicken will gather her young and cover them with her wings. As her chicks nestle under her body for protection from the flames, they are sheltered and kept safe. Once the fire has passed, the chicks emerge alive. The hen, however, in acting as their refuge, perishes. Her sacrifice is ultimate. Her life for theirs. Christ, in like fashion, calls us to find refuge in his mercy and love. Under his wings, we are forgiven, cleansed, and given a new life—blessings we can receive because of his ultimate sacrifice. His life for ours.

Savior, I run to the shelter of your wings! I need your forgiveness and your cleansing, and I desire eternal life. Thank you for your sacrifice. Cover me in your mercy and love.

LOOK UP!

lift up my eyes to the hills—from where will my help come? My help comes from the Lord, who made heaven and earth.... The Lord is your keeper; the Lord is your shade at your right hand. The sun shall not strike you by day, nor the moon by night. The Lord will keep you from all evil; he will keep your life.

Psalm 121:1–2, 5–7

Sunburn! Heat exhaustion! Sunstroke! Ever had the sun strike you? At times, life can be a lot like the scorching sun. We can get weary from the intensity of what we're going through. During such times, however, God's presence is like a shade tree...with a freshwater spring underneath! When we look to him for help, he leads us to a place of reprieve and protection, not just one time, but every time we cry out to him.

Lord, I lift up my eyes to you today. When the intensity of my life becomes unbearable, you alone are my source of shade and refreshment.

Never Forsaken, Never Shaken

God has said, "I will never leave you or forsake you." So we can say with confidence, "The Lord is my helper; I will not be afraid. What can anyone do to me?"

Hebrews 13:5–6

Anyone who has ever been abandoned probably has deep fears that they will be abandoned again. The worm of insecurity can eat away at subsequent relationships, weakening and eventually destroying them. This, in turn, feeds the existing fear. It's a cycle of destruction. That's why God's promise to never leave nor forsake us is such a powerful assurance. When we lay hold of it, God's unfailing presence causes our seedling faith to grow into an unshakable oak.

Father, how I need the security of your presence! Truly, you are the one who will never abandon me. For you will be with me always: in life, in death, and in the life to come.

Lost and Found

$\mathcal{I}$ have gone astray like a lost sheep; seek out your servant, for I do not forget your commandments.
Psalm 119:176

Walking by the big cardboard box in the elementary school office, I saw a sign over it that read "Lost and Found." The box was full of jackets, books, backpacks, shoes, notebooks, action figures, and various other objects. Each item had been lost and was now waiting to be found again. Likely, however, most of the stuff would end up being donated to charity for one of two reasons: either the child had not realized that the item was missing; or, more likely, he or she had given up searching for it. Too bad! Some of those jackets had expensive brand names. How much more valuable we are to God than a brand-name jacket! How diligently he seeks us out during our lifetime, never forgetting, never giving up on us. The real question is this: Are we willing to be found?

Lord, in whatever ways I am lost, please find me.
I am willing to be found.

Praise & Worship

❧ ❧ ❧

PRAISE FOR THE GIFT OF LIFE

You, O Lord, are my hope, my trust, O Lord, from my youth. Upon you I have leaned from my birth; it was you who took me from my mother's womb. My praise is continually of you.

Psalm 71:5–6

At 5:15 on a clear May morning, the midwife laid a brand-new human life on my wife's stomach. My inner being praised God as I shed tears of wonder-filled joy. Later as I reflected on seeing that tiny, naked infant take her first breath of air, I realized that before any of us in the delivery room had the privilege of meeting her, her Creator had spent nine months with her. As I pondered the significance of that one-on-one time in the womb, I prayed that she would always know the peace of God's presence.

Lord of my life, from the beginning you have been with me. May I praise you all of my days!

Sharing Heaven's Praise

*Holy, holy, holy, the Lord God the Almighty,
who was and is and is to come.... You are worthy, our
Lord and God, to receive glory and honor and power,
for you created all things, and by your will they
existed and were created.*

Revelation 4:8, 11

In many and varied ways, creation appeals to our senses—
whether animal, vegetable, or mineral; landscape, seascape,
or skyscape; sight, smell, or touch. Our spirits leap for joy
at our Creator's goodness. Our minds reel as we try
to fathom his genius.

Today, Lord God Almighty, I praise your amazing works!
Thank you for revealing so much about yourself through what
you have made.

THE GOD WHO IS ABLE

Ah Lord God! It is you who made the heavens and the earth by your great power and by your outstretched arm! Nothing is too hard for you.

Jeremiah 32:17

How would you answer this question: Is anything too difficult for God? Now how would you answer this question: Is _____ too difficult for God? (Fill in the blank with your most pressing problem.) Is there a difference between the answers you gave, or is your faith as real for your own circumstances as it is for your creed of beliefs? It can be a struggle to trust when things get frustrating or frightening, but God is not at a loss when it comes to dealing with what seems impossible to us.

Lord, I will put my trust fully in you and declare that nothing, not even _____, is too difficult for you.

Mary's Song

My soul magnifies the Lord, and my spirit rejoices in God my Savior, for he has looked with favor on the lowliness of his servant. Surely, from now on all generations will call me blessed; for the Mighty One has done great things for me, and holy is his name. His mercy is for those who fear him from generation to generation.

Luke 1:46–50

Mary was likely in her teens when this song came streaming from her over-full heart. In her words we find clues as to why, perhaps, God chose her: There is gratitude, humility, joy, a focus on God's character and promises, and concern for the welfare of others. May our own hearts be so full of such true and fitting praise!

Form in me, dear Lord, a pure heart that overflows with praise!

THE BEST THING

Because your steadfast love is better than life, my lips will praise you. So I will bless you as long as I live; I will lift up my hands and call on your name. My soul is satisfied as with a rich feast, and my mouth praises you with joyful lips.

Psalm 63:3–5

In *The Sound of Music*, Maria (played by Julie Andrews) teaches the Von Trapp children to sing a song in praise of their "favorite things." Their list includes "brown paper packages tied up with string," "warm woolen mittens," and "snowflakes that stay on my nose and eyelashes." (Are you humming the tune yet?) Most of us probably have our own list of homespun comforts we could easily splice into that song. And yet, what among these can compare to the love of God? Every comfort is a mere shadow in the warm light of his unfailing love.

My Savior, I will always praise you for loving me. Your love is, indeed, better than life to me!

KEPT IN CHRIST

To him who is able to keep you from falling, and to make you stand without blemish in the presence of his glory with rejoicing, to the only God our Savior, through Jesus Christ our Lord, be glory, majesty, power, and authority, before all time and now and for ever. Amen.

Jude 24–25

Jesus Christ is the one who has made us able to stand in God's presence without fear of condemnation. He is the one whose sacrifice has made a way for us to live with God eternally. When we begin to fear God's punishment, when we begin to doubt God's love, when we begin to look to our own good works as a means of salvation, we must stop immediately, drop these thoughts, and run right back to Christ. In him, only in him, always in him, is where we are kept safe and made fit for eternity.

Jesus, I praise you for making me able to stand in you and not fall!

A Yearning to Worship

How lovely is your dwelling place, O Lord of hosts! My soul longs, indeed it faints for the courts of the Lord; my heart and my flesh sing for joy to the living God. Even the sparrow finds a home, and the swallow a nest for herself, where she may lay her young, at your altars, O Lord of hosts, my King and my God. Happy are those who live in your house, ever singing your praise.

Psalm 84:1–4

How the writer of this psalm loved to praise God! His longing to be in a place where he could join others in worship made his soul feel faint with desire. To him, even the birds who built their nests near God's altar seemed to be singing praises to their Creator...and for all we know, perhaps they were! Do you long to join in the praise as well?

Fill my heart with a yearning to worship you, O Lord!

GOD IS GREAT, GOD IS GOOD

Yours, O Lord, are the greatness, the power, the glory, the victory, and the majesty; for all that is in the heavens and on the earth is yours; yours is the kingdom, O Lord, and you are exalted as head above all. Riches and honor come from you, and you rule over all. In your hand are power and might; and it is in your hand to make great and to give strength to all.

1 Chronicles 29:11–12

Looking at God's tenderness and his greatness can be like looking at a hologram that reveals different pictures, depending on which way you turn it. Of course, God is not like that hologram, since he is always the same; it's just that there is so much to him that we cannot possibly perceive it all at once. How amazing is his power and might, his greatness and majesty! How precious is his tenderness and mercy, his humility and kindness. How blessed we are to be his children!

God of Heaven, I see your greatness and your goodness all around me, and I am filled with awe.

BEYOND BELIEF!

To him who by the power at work within us is able to accomplish abundantly far more than all we can ask or imagine, to him be glory in the church and in Christ Jesus to all generations, for ever and ever. Amen.

Ephesians 3:20–21

Our salvation in Christ is only the beginning of our life in him. God's unbelievable plans for our lives outstrip even our own best ideas and inspirations. The wonderful news is that we don't have to muster extraordinary strength or imagination to fulfill God's extraordinary call. It is his own power that works within us, carrying his purposes to completion. And what may not seem extraordinary to us here and now will be fully revealed in heaven.

Lord, by human standards, my life may not seem extraordinary, but I praise you for your power at work in me, accomplishing your great eternal purposes.

A God for All Peoples

Let the peoples praise you, O God; let all the peoples praise you. Let the nations be glad and sing for joy, for you judge the peoples with equity and guide the nations upon earth.

Psalm 67:3–4

There isn't a person on earth God doesn't want to see enter into the joy and blessing of his kingdom. What is your heritage, your nationality, your culture, your race? God loves you, and he loves your people! He welcomes your praise and the praises of your people. He longs to bless you, and he longs to bless your people. Come worship him today, for your God is a God for all people!

All of us have come from you, O Lord. You have made the people of the earth, and we belong to you. May I praise you with all the people of God today, for you have welcomed us into your kingdom.

Generations to Come

So even to old age and gray hairs, O God, do not forsake me, until I proclaim your might to all the generations to come. Your power and your righteousness, O God, reach the high heavens.

Psalm 71:18

Our habits of prayer and praise are effective ways to communicate the reality of our faith in God to younger generations. Each time we pray with or for a younger person, and each time we point to God by praising his goodness, we make an indelible impression (without the intimidation that lectures or "sermons" can carry). As we openly and yet humbly let our relationship with God shine through, God is able to use that light to draw others to himself.

My Lord, please let my praise of you shine like a light that draws future generations to your love.

Thanksgiving & Gratitude

WHOLEHEARTED THANKS

I give you thanks, O Lord, with my whole heart.... I bow down toward your holy temple and give thanks to your name for your steadfast love and your faithfulness; for you have exalted your name and your word above everything.

Psalm 138:1–2

For those who have spent time studying God's word and calling on his name, two things become abundantly clear: God is unwavering in his love and unparalleled in his faithfulness. Is it not marvelous that the God of heaven offers his love and faithfulness to us, though we cannot match it? He is satisfied with our hearts turning toward him in gratitude to humbly receive what he offers freely.

With my whole heart, Lord, I thank you that I know your faithfulness and your love through your name and word.

Eternal Gratitude

hen the twenty-four elders who sit on their thrones before God fell on their faces and worshipped God, singing, "We give you thanks, Lord God Almighty, who are and who were, for you have taken your great power and begun to reign."
Revelation 11:16–17

Thanksgiving is not limited to one particular day in heaven. No, in heaven thanksgiving is perpetual. Heaven's residents are free of pride, fear, and foolishness—failings that often hinder our gratitude here on earth. In heaven we will clearly see the true nature of things. When this age ends and the next is ushered in, we can be sure that we will join in heaven's eternal gratitude. For then it will be fully revealed to us how right and good, just and merciful, humble and powerful our God is. But, of course, we need not wait until then to begin giving thanks!

Lord God Almighty, rule and reign in my heart today, and let my eternal thanks begin here and now.

Awaking Thanks

Awake, my soul! Awake, O harp and lyre! I will awake the dawn. I will give thanks to you, O Lord, among the peoples.... Be exalted, O God, above the heavens, and let your glory be over all the earth.

Psalm 108:1–3, 5

Over time, our gratitude can become lethargic—like a sleepiness that overtakes our perspective. Perhaps saying grace at meals becomes rote, singing songs of thanksgiving in a worship service evokes no true gratitude, or we meet a wonderful moment in nature with what amounts to a yawn. We need these signs to awaken our hearts to the goodness of God in our lives. Stirring up thanksgiving requires purposefulness, but generally speaking, it does not require great effort. So awake, my soul! Give thanks to God.

You, O Lord, deserve my thanks. I will purpose today to awaken fresh thanksgiving.

INDESCRIBABLE!

Thanks be to God for his indescribable gift!
2 Corinthians 9:15

What an apt word—*indescribable*—to attempt to describe
the nature of God's gift to us. When we read the Gospel
accounts of Jesus' life, death, and resurrection, there really
is no description that could ever do justice to the wonder of
our heavenly Father's plan of salvation brought to us through
his Son, Jesus Christ. He chose to love us all the way to the
Cross. May we never lose our sense of awe at God's great
grace lavished on us.

Heavenly Father, thank you for saving me through your Son,
Jesus. I am thankful that I enjoy a relationship with you through
his sacrifice. Help me share the good news of this
gift with others.

Living Wisdom

It is good to give thanks to the Lord, to sing praises to your name, O Most High; ... For you, O Lord, have made me glad by your work; at the works of your hands I sing for joy. How great are your works, O Lord! Your thoughts are very deep!

Psalm 92:1, 4–5

Daily the sun takes its stroll across the sky. Clouds form and wander about the atmosphere. Animals migrate. Plants and trees dance in the wind. Waters tumble and rush, ebb and flow, swell and break. How clearly God's work in motion testifies to his great, living wisdom! God is not dead nor asleep nor a mere idea. He is real and active in our world. Give him thanks and sing for joy, for his works tell us that he is near, he is attentive, and he is intimately involved with all that he has created.

Thank you, Lord God, for all your works! They speak of your wisdom and bring joy to my heart.

FRAGRANT SAINTS

hanks be to God, who in Christ always leads us in triumphal procession, and through us spreads in every place the fragrance that comes from knowing him.

2 Corinthians 2:14

The attitudes and behaviors of living selfishly, quite frankly, stink. Such selfishness leaves the lingering stench of anger, lying, hatred, bitterness, and impatience. Those belonging to Christ, however, are called to follow him and experience increasing victory over self-centered living. The result is that wherever we go, we should leave a wonderful aroma: the fragrance of love, joy, peace, patience, kindness, goodness, faithfulness, gentleness, and self-control. Thanks to God, we can be washed clean of our stinky selfishness and be made fragrant in Christ Jesus.

Father, thank you for leading me, in your Son, to victory over selfishness. May the fragrance that comes from knowing Christ linger wherever I go.

Because He Is Good

Enter his gates with thanksgiving, and his courts with praise. Give thanks to him, bless his name. For the Lord is good; his steadfast love endures forever, and his faithfulness to all generations.

Psalm 100:4–5

"Because I said so!" As a child, did you ever get that response from a parent or teacher when you asked "why" about one of their directives? "Because I said so" is intended to end the discussion and send the child to do whatever he or she was told. As children of God, we are given much better reasons than "Because I said so" when called to give thanks to our heavenly Father. Because he is good. Because his love endures forever. Because he is always faithful. What a joy to carry out the psalmist's mandates, knowing they are the very things we long to do in light of our Father's goodness to us!

I have many reasons to give you thanks this day, Father. Your goodness is just the first one on my list.

Daniel's Prayer of Thanks

o you, O God of my ancestors, I give thanks and praise, for you have given me wisdom and power, and have now revealed to me what we asked of you, for you have revealed to us what the king ordered.

Daniel 2:23

Daniel was in a tight spot. He needed God's wisdom—to be shown the king's dream and its interpretation—or he would be executed along with all the other wise men in Babylon. Immediately Daniel began to pray and ask God for the answers he needed. As I try to imagine what it would have been like to be Daniel, I marvel at his faith and bravery. He prayed for extraordinary wisdom from God, received it, and then had the presence of heart and mind to stop and give thanks to God before rushing in to the king with his answer.

Father, I often ask you for things in the heat of the moment, in the urgency of my need. Help me be as quick to give you thanks for the answers you send.

Resurrection of Joy

You have turned my mourning into dancing; you have taken off my sackcloth and clothed me with joy, so that my soul may praise you and not be silent. O Lord my God, I will give thanks to you forever.
Psalm 30:11–12

Have you ever entered into a darkness of soul from which you thought you would never emerge? In this passage, the presence of a sackcloth garment signifies a season of mourning—a time when grief has gripped the heart and won't let go. Perhaps you are going through such a time right now, and it seems that nothing can bring you back into the sunlight of life again. Don't lose faith! God is able to heal your heart, causing joy to return, dancing to resume, and thanksgiving to fall again from your lips.

Gracious Lord, when my heart is too heavy with grief to find a song of praise, please resurrect my joy that I may again give thanks to your name.

GATEWAY TO THANKS

*Open to me the gates of righteousness, that I may enter through them and give thanks to the Lord....
I thank you that you have answered me and have become my salvation.*

Psalm 118:19, 21

It's interesting to note that when we are not walking in the ways of God, we are unwilling (or perhaps unable) to give him proper thanks. When we're doing our own thing, we tend to grumble and groan our way through the day rather than thank and praise our God. When we purpose to walk in God's ways and listen to his voice, however, we are filled with so much gratitude and joy that thanksgiving becomes second nature. If we've wandered away from the gate of righteousness that leads to thanksgiving, let's stop this very second and turn back. The gate is before us now—it's time to enter in.

Lord, free my heart from things that would lead me away from the gate of righteousness. May I enter through that gate today and give you thanks, because you alone are my salvation.

THE BEST IS YET TO COME

When this perishable body puts on imperishability, and this mortal body puts on immortality, then the saying that is written will be fulfilled: "Death has been swallowed up in victory." … [T]hanks be to God, who gives us the victory through our Lord Jesus Christ.

1 Corinthians 15:54, 57

Of all the things for which we have to be grateful in this life, one of the most encouraging for us as children of God is that the best is yet to come. Our time here is just a warm-up for what lies ahead. Everything on this earth that is marked by decay, decline, disease, and death will no longer exist in heaven. God will bring Christ's victory to fullness when he does away with the old and ushers us into the new. Give thanks with all your heart today, for no matter what your pain, loss, failure, or fear might be, in Christ you have a glorious future!

Dear Lord, grant that I may keep an eternal perspective from which I can thank you for the best that is yet to come.

Forgiveness & Repentance

WASHED CLEAN

Have mercy on me, O God, according to your steadfast love; according to your abundant mercy blot out my transgressions. Wash me thoroughly from my iniquity and cleanse me from my sin.

Psalm 51:1–2

Since we stumble in many ways, we frequently need God's mercy to bathe us. The good news is that our Lord's mercies are new every morning, which means fresh bathwater, so to speak, when we go to him for cleansing of our sins. Our part is going to him dirt and all, asking to become clean. His part is faithfully keeping his promise to wash away the dirt. If you're feeling in need of a spiritual bath today, go to him. He will cleanse you.

O God, I seek your mercy and love. Thank you for receiving my confession and for washing me clean of my sins.

READY TO FORGIVE

You are a God ready to forgive, gracious and merciful, slow to anger and abounding in steadfast love.

Nehemiah 9:17

"Ready!...Set!...Go!" These words are often heard on the playground. They are the words to start a race. A noisy mob of kids always becomes quiet, anticipating the word "Go!" and wanting to be the first to take off. And like so many tightly coiled springs, the runners are poised and quivering at the starting line. This is the picture of readiness we can call to mind when we hear of God's readiness to forgive us. Like a runner in the starting block, God is poised, waiting for us to give him the go-ahead to intervene with his grace and forgiveness when we have sinned. He's ready even now.

How eager and quick you are to forgive, Father! Help me to be as quick to confess my need for your mercy as you are to give it.

WHEN WE'VE BROUGHT IT ON OURSELVES

Relieve the troubles of my heart, and bring me out of my distress. Consider my affliction and my trouble, and forgive all my sins.

Psalm 25:17–18

A young woman, now in her thirties, struggles with the consequences of a bad decision she made a few years ago. Despite warnings from friends, she married a man whose track record was openly inconsistent. Within two months of saying their vows, he was disappearing for days at a time. "I brought it on myself," she says now as she struggles to piece her life back together. One of the amazing things she's discovering about God, however, is that he is willing to help his children even when they *have* "brought it on themselves." He does not chide with "I told you so" but forgives us and leads us back into his good purposes for our lives. Consequences may remain, but he turns even those into ways of demonstrating his grace.

Father, help me, by faith, to accept your complete forgiveness and your invitation to move on.

When Sin Overwhelms

O you who answer prayer! ... When deeds of iniquity overwhelm us, you forgive our transgressions.
Psalm 65:2–3

Ever been in a funk? A place of discouragement and blahness that you just can't shake? Those times seem to make us prime targets for an ambush of shame. Shame comes slinking into our thoughts and emotions, diligently reminding us of all of our failures, sins, skeletons, and despicable tendencies. Shame shouts, "You're stupid! You're ugly! You're bad! You're unlovable!" And just when we need God most, we feel certain he does not love us. But shame is a liar, especially when it tells us we're unlovable, for there is one who loves us unconditionally and forgives us completely. All we have to do is ask.

Father, please chase away the shame that lingers in my soul and reminds me of my many sins and failures. Overwhelm me with your forgiveness and love as I run to you.

FORGIVENESS TO GOD'S GLORY

Help us, O God of our salvation, for the glory of your name; deliver us, and forgive our sins, for your name's sake.

Psalm 79:9

One day when I was little, our family was having Sunday dinner at my grandparents' home, and I lied to Grandma. Taking me aside, my dad let me know that I had a spanking coming when we got home. From that moment on, I could think of nothing else. Later when we arrived home, I followed Dad to collect my spanking. But instead of asking me the usual question—"Do you know why you're getting this spanking?"—he picked up a roll of candy and invited me to sit next to him and talk about what happened. Since I was trying to hold back sobs, I couldn't eat the candy he offered me, but for the first time in spanking matters, he was extending mercy and forgiveness to me. How much easier it would later be for me to grasp the concept of God's mercy and to accept his forgiveness. What a glorious heavenly Father we have!

I will always tell of your forgiveness, Lord, to the glory of your name!

Forgiven Soul, Reverent Heart

If you, O Lord, should mark iniquities ... who could stand? But there is forgiveness with you, so that you may be revered.

Psalm 130:3–4

Those who understand God's forgiveness most, worship him best. A clear example in Scripture is the account of the sinful woman who washed Jesus' feet with her tears as Simon the Pharisee looked on in disgust. Jesus, knowing Simon's thoughts, used an illustration to illuminate the situation. A moneylender, Jesus told Simon, forgave two debts, one large and one small. "Who do you suppose loved the moneylender more?" Jesus asked Simon. Simon answered that it would likely be the one who had owed the greater amount. Jesus affirmed Simon's answer and brought the point home. Simon, whose sins were small in his own eyes, had not offered Jesus even the customary courtesy of water for washing his feet. The woman, on the other hand, who had been forgiven of great sin washed his feet with her hair and tears as an act of love.

Lord, may I perceive how much I have been forgiven and love you accordingly.

THE GROUND OF FORGIVENESS

We do not present our supplication before you on the ground of our righteousness, but on the ground of your great mercies. O Lord, hear; O Lord, forgive; O Lord, listen and act and do not delay!

Daniel 9:18–19

Have you ever been tempted to think that God's goodness to you is based on what a likable person you are? It sounds kind of silly, but if we're honest with ourselves, we sometimes harbor thoughts of being buddies with God in a way that others are not. This "teacher's pet" syndrome doesn't really hold water, though, in light of Scripture. There is one reason why God is good to us, why he shows mercy, why he forgives; that reason is that he is always good and merciful. All anyone has to do is turn to him, and he will help and forgive.

O God, I'm so glad that your mercy and forgiveness aren't offered on the basis of my merits but are anchored in your love.

Using the Big Bucket

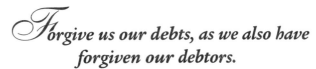

*orgive us our debts, as we also have
forgiven our debtors.*

Matthew 6:12

Scripture makes it quite clear that God will show each of us
mercy in proportion to how merciful we are toward others.
What a great way to encourage mercy among his children! If
I use a big bucket of mercy in my relationships with others,
God will get out the big bucket in my relationship with him.
If I use the thimble, he will do likewise. How much mercy do
I want from God? I need to show him by giving to others in
the way I would have him give to me.

Lord, I need the big bucket of mercy from you, not the thimble.
Please help me throw away my thimble and always carry
a big bucket for others.

U-TURN TO FORGIVENESS

Hide your face from my sins, and blot out all my iniquities. Create in me a clean heart, O God, and put a new and right spirit within me.

Psalm 51:9–10

If I'm driving east on Interstate 90 from Chicago, I'll never get to Seattle. It doesn't matter how many people I convince to the contrary, I won't arrive in the Emerald City until I turn my car around and start driving west. It's the same kind of thing when we're going our own way and insisting that we're going to arrive in the middle of God's will for our lives. Until we turn around and start going God's way, there's no chance of experiencing the good plans and purposes that he desires for us. The good news is that, if we do find ourselves going the wrong way, God's forgiveness and the right direction are just a U-turn away.

I want to move in the direction of your will, Lord. Please show me any U-turns I need to make today.

Heart Inspection

But who can detect their errors? Clear me from hidden faults.... Then I shall be blameless, and innocent of great transgression.
Psalm 19:12–13

When I'm not wearing my glasses, my house looks pretty tidy. The carpets look free of debris; the sinks and faucets seem sparkly; and the dusting can wait another week. But I get a very different perspective once I don my specs. How did I not see the crumbs I left on the rug from those crackers I ate the night before? What's with the toothpaste spots all over the bathroom sink? And heavens! I could draw a big smiley face in the dust on the bookshelf. Attempts to judge my own character are very much like my inability to judge the cleanliness of my house without the aid of corrective lenses. We'll miss things if we rely on our human perspective. But when we invite God to do the inspection, he sees clearly, giving us a thorough cleansing from our sin.

Come inspect my heart, Lord God, and cleanse me of sins
I have overlooked.

SIN FORGIVEN AND FORGOTTEN

Do not remember the sins of my youth or my transgressions; according to your steadfast love remember me, for your goodness' sake, O Lord!

Psalm 25:7

I don't like to remember the sins of my youth. Fortunately God doesn't either. His word tells us that he casts our sins away from him as far as the east is from the west. That's a great promise in my thinking, because I don't want to meet up with those sins—or any of my sins for that matter—ever again. I'm grateful for a God who is so willing to forgive and forget, whether I've confessed a sin 50 years ago or a sin just this morning.

Thank you for your forgiveness and for forgetting as well, my Lord. Help me learn to forgive myself and others that way too.

No Hiding

Iacknowledged my sin to you, and I did not hide my iniquity; I said, "I will confess my transgressions to the Lord," and you forgave the guilt of my sin.

Psalm 32:5

Trying to hide our sin from God is like trying to hide a lump of Limburger cheese in our pocket. Not only is it pointless, it's also unwise. Since God sees and knows everything about us at all times, our best course of action is always to go to him right away, confess our sin, and receive his forgiveness. Once that is done, he can help us pick up the pieces, conquer the habit, or do whatever is necessary to get headed in the right direction. The longer we wait, the stinkier things get. Time to empty our pockets!

Lord, you know everything about me. I may hide my sin from others, but you see it clearly. Please set me free from the guilt of my sin as I confess it to you right now.

Mercy & Comfort

HELP FOR THE UNDERDOG

O Lord, you will hear the desire of the meek; you will strengthen their heart, you will incline your ear to do justice for the orphan and the oppressed.

Psalm 10:17–18

We tend to be drawn to stories about the "underdog" coming out on top. Perhaps it's because God has poured his own mercy into our hearts for those who are most vulnerable. So whenever we offer help and comfort to the helpless, we are carrying out God's work in this world. Are there "underdogs" in your life? Perhaps an elderly relative or friend, a troubled child, or someone with a physical or mental disability? Whenever you reach out to help them, you are giving them refreshment from the well of God's merciful heart and carrying out some of his most cherished work.

Merciful Lord, use me today to offer your comfort to the humble and helpless.

A Return to Mercy

*he Lord your God is gracious and merciful,
and will not turn away his face from you,
if you return to him.*

2 Chronicles 30:9

When we've lapsed back into an attitude or behavior we
know is not pleasing to God, often our impulse is to avoid
him and stop praying and reading his word. We may feel
ashamed and certain that he'd rather not listen to us, but
nothing could be further from the truth. Second Chronicles
spells it out in no uncertain terms: God's mercy doesn't wear
out. He waits for us, and his gracious heart is wide open and
ready to receive us if we will only return to him.

When I feel like avoiding you, Lord, remind me that your mercy
is waiting for me.

MERCY FOR GOD'S SERVANTS

O Lord, let your ear be attentive to the prayer of your servant, and to the prayer of your servants who delight in revering your name. Give success to your servant today, and grant him mercy.

Nehemiah 1:11

Nehemiah prayed this prayer as a Jewish exile working as a cupbearer in a pagan king's court. He was about to go before the king to make a petition on behalf of his people—that they might be permitted to rebuild the ruins of Jerusalem and its temple. It was a crazy request, but it was the burning desire of Nehemiah's heart to see the Lord's name lifted up once again among his people. God gave Nehemiah the mercy he needed from the king, and then some! Jerusalem and the temple were rebuilt with supplies provided by the king. What "crazy" desire is in your heart for carrying out God's work on earth? May he grant it to you, according to his great mercy.

I love to see you honored, Lord. Please open the doors to me for making your name known to those around me.

The Lord's Prayer

Our Father in heaven, hallowed be your name. Your kingdom come. Your will be done, on earth as it is in heaven. Give us this day our daily bread. And forgive us our debts, as we also have forgiven our debtors. And do not bring us to the time of trial, but rescue us from the evil one.

Matthew 6:9–13

Our Lord was teaching his followers how to pray when he gave this example to them. Beautiful in its simplicity, reverent, humble, and honest, it remains a comforting and reassuring model for Christians everywhere. Many have found enrichment and insight as they've taken time to ponder each line. And yet even a child can understand its basic truth and come to understand the comfort and mercy of our heavenly Father.

Continue to teach me to pray, dear Lord, and reveal your comfort and mercy to me.

MERCIFUL PROTECTION

Be merciful to me, O God, . . . in the shadow of your wings I will take refuge, until the destroying storms pass by.

Psalm 57:1

An icy blast had blown down from Alaska through the West Coast. It was a "freak storm," and the temperatures plummeted as the winds rose. I was working the graveyard shift that night when I received a call from my mom. She was hiding under a kitchen table, frightened for her life as she heard and felt the massive evergreen trees in our yard crashing to the ground all around. Because of the widespread power outages, Dad had been called to his job at the utility company, and so, at midnight, Mom found herself alone in the darkness, praying that God would keep her safe until the storm's fury passed. When I finally made it home, Mom was unharmed. Trees had fallen all around, but by God's mercy alone, it seemed, none had touched the house.

Father, protect me with your mercy, I pray, from the "storms" I'm facing that frighten me and threaten my well-being.

Mercy Received

Return, O my soul, to your rest, for the Lord has dealt bountifully with you.

Psalm 116:7

When we're praying for God's mercy, waiting for relief from some trouble or difficulty, it can seem like an eternity since we experienced peace of mind. While we're in this "waiting room" of God's timing, we can draw strength and comfort by remembering the ways in which the Lord has "dealt bountifully" with us, the ways he's rescued us and come through with protection and provision when we've needed it, the ways he's resolved conflict and restored relationships. As our minds return to his acts of mercy, our souls can return to their rest, for God has and always will deal bountifully with his children.

Even as I wait for your mercy, Lord, I will find rest and comfort, remembering mercies I have already received.

Comforting Presence

*Even though I walk through the darkest valley,
I fear no evil; for you are with me; your rod and your
staff—they comfort me.*

Psalm 23:4

It was late in December when I drove over the mountains to visit friends in Calgary. The short winter day was made shorter when I headed into a mountain pass as the sun was going down. Soon it was pitch-black, and I couldn't see the lines on the winding mountain road. Huge semitrucks zoomed past my small car, throwing slush and road debris all over my windshield. I wanted to stop my car, but I could not see if there was anywhere to pull over. To keep myself on the road when the trucks passed, I focused on the red blur of their taillights. But mostly, I prayed because even in the dark valley of that mountain pass, I was not alone. Indeed, it is my comfort always to know that I am never alone.

I long to be comforted, Lord. Teach me to find it in your company, for you are with me in all places at all times.

COMFORT IN GOD'S PROMISES

This is my comfort in my distress, that your promise gives me life.

Psalm 119:50

Broken promises are deeply painful. Disappointment, shame, fear, mistrust, anger, grudges, even estrangement can come from someone not keeping his or her word. We've all had someone break a promise made to us, and on the flip side, most of us have broken a promise to someone else. If enough promises are broken—whether our own or those of the other person—what was a close relationship will invariably fracture. Trust may die and, with it, hope. But there is One who has never broken a promise and who never will. His promises bring trust and hope back to life in us, comforting and healing our aching hearts.

It's true, Lord, broken promises have wounded me. Please come and heal my heart, reviving my trust and renewing my hope as I place my faith in your promises.

COMFORT IN GOD'S RULES

*hen I think of your ordinances from of old,
I take comfort, O Lord.*

Psalm 119:52

Imagine playing a game of checkers without any rules. The ensuing small-scale chaos would render the game meaningless. Rules provide a common purpose, a common ground for accomplishing that purpose, and the rewarding satisfaction of knowing when you have attained your goal. God's ordinances, or laws, provide the rules that we need to be able to enjoy meaning and purpose in our lives. They comfort us in ways we aren't even aware of but would quickly notice if they were taken away. Some people wrongly assume that removing God's rules from their lives will bring them freedom, but the kind of freedom they are seeking is not found outside the rules. It is found in relationship with God, who made the rules for our comfort.

Lord, thank you for the comfort that comes from keeping your
rules and from knowing that you are keeping me
as I walk in them.

THE COMFORT OF GOD'S LOVE

Let your steadfast love become my comfort
according to your promise to your servant.
Psalm 119:76

We value the loving word that comes to us from a cherished friend, a child, a sibling, a spouse. But when we hear messages of God's love, they sometimes fall flat on our ears instead of stirring our heart with joy. It's important to know that until we come to know and value God's love, we will be missing out on the best of all loves. God's love is perfect and powerful; it is the pure source of the diluted versions we find in human love. Despite what mistaken notions or conclusions we may have about God based on past experience, his is not a heart of stale sermons nor the face of severe religion. His is the heart of love, joy, and peace; the face of patience, kindness, and goodness; the strength of faithfulness, humility, and self-control. There is no love more valuable, no love more comforting.

Stir my heart to pursue your love, Lord, that I might always know its joys and comforts.

Strong in Christ's Comfort

Now may our Lord Jesus Christ himself and God our Father, who loved us and through grace gave us eternal comfort and good hope, comfort your hearts and strengthen them in every good work and word.

2 Thessalonians 2:16–17

Who better than we—we who have been on the receiving end of God's grace and have experienced his "eternal comfort and good hope"—to dispense his love, grace, and comfort to the world around us? "Every good work and word" we do in his strength will carry the stamp of his love. Every person we reach out to will be touched by his comforting presence. We don't need special programs or perfect presentation to carry out his work, only trust that the one who has already brought his comfort to our hearts can bring it to others through us.

I'm so grateful for your comforting presence in my life, dear Lord. Fill me, I pray, with your strength and grace that, through me, others may come to know you as well.

Hope & Healing

❧ ❧ ❧

One Who Loves Us

Turn, O Lord, save my life; deliver me for the sake of your steadfast love.

Psalm 6:4

The most vital healing we will ever receive is the new life Christ brings us through his death and resurrection. Even if our bodies remain broken during this lifetime, we know from Scripture that they will be made glorious in heaven. If our spirits are not made alive through God's saving grace, however, all is lost. Because of his steadfast love, God sent his only begotten Son to save us. Because of his steadfast love, God pursues us and calls us into his kingdom. And because of his steadfast love, God heals us through the salvation we have in Christ.

Gracious Father, I receive your ultimate healing for me in Christ—your salvation that has come to me because of your steadfast love.

One Who Helps and Heals

Lord my God, I cried to you for help, and you have healed me.

Psalm 30:2

My nephew apparently has a high pain tolerance. He broke his arm badly when he was about nine years old, and no one realized it for several minutes because he didn't cry out. We might have chalked it up to shock, but at no time did he behave like someone in great pain. Another time, a six-inch-long, half-inch-wide chunk of wood from a split-rail fence lodged deeply in the underside of his upper arm, requiring surgical removal and several stitches. Again, through the entire ordeal, he never cried out. Of course, we tend to admire tough people, but when it comes to matters of physical, emotional, or spiritual healing, we often cheat ourselves by not calling out to God for help. He's willing to help us, especially when we ask him for the help we need.

Father, I'm sorry for trying to be tough so much of the time. I'm your child, and I need your help and your healing.

Blessing and Being Blessed

Happy are those who consider the poor; the Lord delivers them in the day of trouble. The Lord protects them and keeps them alive; they are called happy in the land.

Psalm 41:1–2

There was an elderly widow who always looked out for her neighbors. She made sure that they had chicken soup when they were sick, food from her farm if they were running low on groceries, and company if they were lonely. Her resources were limited, but what she had, she gave. When her own health began to fail, it looked as if she would be isolated since she no longer lived near her family. With God's help, however, all the love and attention she had offered so many others fell on her like a gentle rain—a rain that fell continuously until she needed it no more.

Lord, help me to be your hands of help and healing to everyone within my reach.

Prayer in Suffering

O Lord, ... restore me to health and make me live! Surely it was for my welfare that I had great bitterness; but you have held back my life from the pit of destruction.... The living, the living, they thank you, as I do this day.

Isaiah 38:16–17, 19

If the Book of Job teaches us anything, it is that we may not be able to discern the reasons or purposes for our pain. In the midst of suffering, though, we can and must keep praying. Prayer may appear futile when we don't receive the relief we're asking for in what we feel is a timely manner. But seeking God—persisting in the belief that he loves us even when everything we're experiencing seems to mock our faith—is far from futile. It is what strengthens our trust, making it unbreakable. So keep praying, keep asking to be healed, and keep faith in God. He's with you—and for you—forever.

O Lord God! I am suffering; please come to my aid. Sustain my faith and heal my body, I pray.

Return to Faith

Return, O faithless children, I will heal your faithlessness. "Here we come to you; for you are the Lord our God.... Truly in the Lord our God is the salvation of [His people]."
Jeremiah 3:22–23

"Parenting is a thankless job," my friend would occasionally sigh. I would smile at her sympathetically. She had three teenagers who usually thought they knew more than she did about life. The deep faith they'd had in her wisdom as children had given way to a persistent skepticism. She was looking out for their well-being, but they thought she was just trying to control them. Over the past decade, trial and error has ushered the teens into their twenties, and trust in their mom has come full circle, renewed by an understanding that she does know more about life and she is for them, not against them.

Father, heal my faithlessness when I don't trust your wisdom and love for me. I will return to you, God of my salvation, and be healed.

BETTER THAN THE BEST

Heal me, O Lord, and I shall be healed; save me, and I shall be saved; for you are my praise.
Jeremiah 17:14

This prayer may seem senselessly redundant, and its significance may escape us unless we pause to consider it further. Do you have a favorite doctor, dentist, mechanic, or hairdresser? A professional who has a proven track record and whom you trust like no one else? You might say, "When Doctor Alexander diagnoses my problem, I can be sure I've been diagnosed properly!" or "When McIntosh repairs my car, it's been repaired. End of car trouble!" We can likewise be sure that no one heals nor saves like our God. In fact, no one truly heals nor saves *except* our God.

You are the one I seek for my healing and salvation, Lord God. No one but you will do for me.

Healing the Wounds of Sin

Come, let us return to the Lord; for it is he who has torn, and he will heal us; he has struck down, and he will bind us up.

Hosea 6:1

In our youth we usually think of sin as something naughty. In our adult years we realize that sin is deadly. Persistent sin kills us—body, soul, and spirit . . . some sins faster than others. God's hope for us, however, is that the cancer of sin not destroy us. Sometimes he takes drastic measures to steer us away from it in his efforts to save us, and sometimes, because of our stubbornness, we get hurt in the process of being saved. In a nutshell, God's plan is to rescue us from sin and then heal us from any damage we may have incurred in the process.

Father, help me let go of sin, return to you, and be healed.

To God's Glory

Sovereign Lord, who made the heaven and the earth, the sea, and everything in them, ... grant to your servants to speak your word with all boldness, while you stretch out your hand to heal.

Acts 4:24, 29–30

Healing is one way God reveals Christ's love and power to those around us. When we tell how the Lord touched our bodies (our heart, mind, soul, or spirit as well), it points people in his direction. They may not acknowledge him right then and there, but it plants a seed of truth in their hearts that can germinate and grow. It's right and good for us to ask God to reveal himself and his glory through healing. For when people see what he has done, it's difficult to deny that he is real.

Help me seek your glory when I seek your healing, heavenly Father. In Jesus' name.

Sin's Hindrance to a Healthy Life

Therefore confess your sins to one another, and pray for one another, so that you may be healed. The prayer of the righteous is powerful and effective.

James 5:16

It's true that sin can damage our health. Generally speaking, sin causes conflict within ourselves and in our relationships with God and others, conflict causes stress, and stress is detrimental to health. Some sins quickly affect our health. Others take a long time to catch up with us. But we can be sure that all sins have a poison somewhere in them. Sin is always a hindrance to a healthy life.

Father, help me confess my sins sooner rather than later. I don't ever want sin to damage my health.

THE BLESSING OF WELL-BEING

Beloved, I pray that all may go well with you and that you may be in good health, just as it is well with your soul.

3 John 2

What a wonderful, grace-filled prayer the apostle John lifted to God for his fellow Christians! Even though suffering can bring spiritual growth and lessons of perseverance, we need not seek out suffering and trials. When all is said and done, God wants to pour out his blessing on us and grant us eternal peace along with unmitigated joy. Imagine! But for now, the apostle's benediction is a small foretaste of God's purposes for us. May we remain faithful to him until he returns.

My gracious heavenly Father, let this prayer cover me, body and soul, today and every day. Amen.

Blessing & Benediction

❧ ❧ ❧

BENEDICTION OF PEACE

The Lord bless you and keep you; the Lord make his face to shine upon you, and be gracious to you; the Lord lift up his countenance upon you, and give you peace.

Numbers 6:24–26

We all crave peace: peace in our world, peace in our relationships, and peace in our own heart and mind. Most of all, we crave peace with God. The blessing of true peace finds its source in God. He created a peaceful world until sin brought strife and turmoil. In response, he sent his Son to make peace again. Now, those who are in Christ know the peace of God. May the blessing of God's peace through Jesus Christ be yours today and always!

In this troubled world, Lord, make me an ambassador of your blessing of peace.

THE FAVOR OF GOD

You bless the righteous, O Lord; you cover them
with favor as with a shield.

Psalm 5:12

What a great blessing! Who would not want God's favor
to be with them—to cover them like a shield? But who are
"the righteous"? Of course, those who have put their trust in
Christ for salvation stand securely in his righteousness. They
are placed in right standing before God by his grace through
their faith. The righteousness that flows to us from that
miracle of grace, however, also needs to flow down into our
everyday living. Elsewhere in Scripture (such as in
Micah 6:8) we're given three simple principles to live by,
which, if followed, guide us into righteous living: to do what
is just; to love kindness by extending it to others;
and to walk humbly with our God.

Father, thank you for the blessing of your favor on my life.
By your grace, please lead me into righteous living through
your word and by your Spirit.

BENEDICTION OF UNITY

May the God of steadfastness and encouragement grant you to live in harmony with one another, in accordance with Christ Jesus, so that together you may with one voice glorify the God and Father of our Lord Jesus Christ.

Romans 15:5–6

Scripture tells us we are called to be at peace with others, especially with those who love and follow Christ. When we've tried our best, though, and have done everything we know to do and unity still seems far off, we can keep trusting "the God of steadfastness and encouragement" who can work in hearts and minds to bring about harmony. Of course, in heaven, all of us who are in Christ will unite our hearts and voices to glorify God. How wonderful it would be if we could make a beginning of it here on earth!

God of peace, inasmuch as it depends on me, help me to be at peace with others, especially with fellow Christians. Where disunity is disturbing my heart, please give me peace as I trust in you to help us work things out in your time.

BENEDICTION OF FREEDOM

Grace to you and peace from God our Father and the Lord Jesus Christ, who gave himself for our sins to set us free from the present evil age, according to the will of our God and Father, to whom be the glory for ever and ever. Amen.

Galatians 1:3–5

Sometimes it can seem as if evil has suddenly risen up to devour civilization, but "this present evil age" existed even in the apostle Paul's day. Jesus himself taught his disciples to pray, "Deliver us from evil." We don't usually think of ourselves as part of the problem of evil, but we are! Or, rather, we are until we experience the power of Christ setting us free from the power of sin. God's grace pulls us from the downward spiral of our participation in this world's ways. Do we still stumble into sin? Yes, like tottering children learning to walk, we fall down. But, in Christ, God puts the desire in us to get up off the filthy floor of sin and to stand upright.

Thank you, Jesus, for the blessing of freedom from the power of sin.

THE BLESSING OF INTEGRITY

Those who have clean hands and pure hearts, who do not lift up their souls to what is false, and do not swear deceitfully. They will receive blessing from the Lord, and vindication from the God of their salvation.

Psalm 24:4–5

We look for honesty and trustworthiness in our relationships with others, don't we? When God relates to us, he looks for those qualities, too. The wonderful thing about a relationship with God, though, is that he doesn't judge us on appearances. In 1 Samuel 16:7, we learn that God's not fooled by how things look from the outside; he looks directly into the heart of a person and knows what's really there. That's a comfort when we're misunderstood, misjudged, or falsely accused. God knows the truth about us, and when we walk in integrity, blessing and vindication will follow.

I want to walk in the blessings of integrity, Lord. Cause me to hold tightly to purity and truth. Where I have been misjudged, misunderstood, or falsely accused, I will trust you to vindicate me.

BENEDICTION OF PRESERVATION

May the God of peace himself sanctify you entirely; and may your spirit and soul and body be kept sound and blameless at the coming of our Lord Jesus Christ.

1 Thessalonians 5:23

Cryogenic freezing is a reality in our world today. Some people choose to have their bodies preserved in this way so that if science should ever learn to resurrect them, they could live again on this earth. Chilling! A much better option, it seems, is to place our trust in God, who gave us life in the first place. His method of preservation is through Christ, who has already been resurrected. Christ promises that we will live with him eternally in a place that cannot be compared to this earth because of its surpassing splendor. Preserved in Christ—spirit, soul, and body until he comes again—is a blessing to us from God's warm heart.

I choose the warmth of your blessing in Christ to preserve me until your Son comes again.

The Blessing of Provision

he earth has yielded its increase; God, our God, has blessed us. May God continue to bless us; let all the ends of the earth revere him.

Psalm 67:6–7

Shelter, clothing, food. These, our Lord told us, the Father knows we have need of, and we should not spend time worrying about them. As you take inventory of your life, can you recall any times when you were utterly without these things? Even a boiled potato is food for a hungry stomach. Even wearing the same two outfits is clothing. Even a couch at a friend's house is shelter. But if we may have had little at times, how much more of our life has been spent enjoying an abundance? How faithful God has been in his promise for provision!

I count my blessings today, Lord, beginning with the clothes I'm wearing, the food set before me, and the roof over my head!

BENEDICTION OF GOOD WORKS

Now may the God of peace, who brought back from the dead our Lord Jesus ... make you complete in everything good so that you may do his will, working among us that which is pleasing in his sight, through Jesus Christ, to whom be the glory for ever and ever. Amen.

Hebrews 13:20–21

Contrary to popular belief, good works by themselves don't get anyone into heaven; only faith in Christ can save us. But faith without works, the apostle James wrote, is dead. It may seem confusing at first glance, but soon we come to realize that faith and good works are linked much like a horse and carriage in the song "Love and Marriage": "You can't have one without the other." Faith comes first and then, by the power of Christ working in us, good works—the kind that please God—begin to manifest. Our desires undergo transformation; our will lines up with God's, and we enjoy the blessing of genuine faith in action.

Father, may my faith in you produce the blessing of good works by the power of Christ at work in me.

BENEDICTION OF ANSWERED PRAYER

*May [the Lord] grant you your heart's desire,
and fulfill all your plans.... May the Lord fulfill
all your petitions.*

Psalm 20:4–5

After being tucked in one night, a little girl prayed fervently before going to sleep that God would let her wake up in her cousin's body to live her cousin's life. This envied cousin lived on a beautiful farm and had a horse. In the morning, upon waking in her own bed, still herself, the girl felt a pang of disappointment. Yet, years later as an adult, she found herself atop a horse on a trail ride with a friend. Remembering that childish prayer, she smiled and took quick inventory of her life. In those moments she realized that she wouldn't want to trade places with anyone. Over the years, God had fulfilled the desire of her little-girl heart, despite the foolishness of her initial request. As a grown-up she was enjoying the wonder of life—her very own life—in full
and meaningful ways.

Thank you, Lord, for the blessing of your faithfulness and
goodness in answering my prayers.

THE BEATITUDES

Blessed are the poor in spirit, for theirs is the kingdom of heaven. Blessed are those who mourn, for they will be comforted. Blessed are the meek, for they will inherit the earth. Blessed are those who hunger and thirst for righteousness, for they will be filled. Blessed are the merciful, for they will receive mercy. Blessed are the pure in heart, for they will see God. Blessed are the peacemakers, for they will be called children of God. Blessed are those who are persecuted for righteousness' sake, for theirs is the kingdom of heaven.

Matthew 5:3–10

Here on earth we tend to think of blessing in terms of power, talent, and wealth. Jesus turned this notion on its head when he opened his Sermon on the Mount by saying that the downtrodden—those who long for and do what is right and good—are those who will inherit lasting blessings.

Father, the "blessings" of this world are passing shadows compared to the eternal blessings we will enjoy if we seek your kingdom and your righteousness above all things.